# Prayers

# for Children

Edited by

## REV. VICTOR HOAGLAND, C.P.

Illustrated by

## WILLIAM LUBEROFF

## THE REGINA PRESS
### NEW YORK

Artwork © Reproducta NY 1997
Text © The Regina Press

# Prayers

## THE SIGN OF THE CROSS

In the name of the Father, and of the Son, and of the Holy Spirit. Amen.

## GLORY BE

Glory to the Father and to the Son and to the Holy Spirit: as it was in the beginning, is now and will be for ever. Amen.

## GRACE BEFORE MEALS

Bless us, O Lord, and these your gifts which we are about to receive from Your bounty, through Christ our Lord. Amen.

## GRACE AFTER MEALS

We give you thanks, almighty God, for these and all your gifts which we have received through Christ our Lord. Amen.

## THE OUR FATHER

Our Father, who art in heaven,
hallowed be thy name.
Thy kingdom come.
Thy will be done on earth,
as it is in heaven.
Give us this day our daily bread,
and forgive us our trespasses,
as we forgive those
who trespass against us,
and lead us not into temptation,
but deliver us from evil. Amen.

## THE HAIL MARY

Hail Mary, full of grace,
the Lord is with you;
blessed are you among women,
and blessed is the fruit
of thy womb, Jesus.
Holy Mary, Mother of God,
pray for us sinners now
and at the hour of our death. Amen.

## ACT OF FAITH

O my God, I believe that you are
one God in three Divine Persons:
Father, Son and Holy Spirit.
I believe that your Divine Son
became man and died for our sins,
and that he will come again to
judge the living and the dead.
I believe these and all the truths
that the Catholic Church teaches,
because you have revealed them,
who can neither deceive nor
be deceived. Amen.

## Act of Hope

O my God, relying on your almighty
power and infinite mercy
and promises, I hope to obtain
pardon of my sins, the help
of your grace and life everlasting
through the merits of Jesus Christ,
my Lord and Redeemer. Amen.

## Act of Love

O my God, I love you above all things
with my whole heart and soul,
because you are all good
and worthy of all love.
I love my neighbor as myself
for the love of you.
I forgive all who have injured me
and ask pardon of all
whom I have injured. Amen.

# The Apostles' Creed

I believe in God, the Father almighty,
creator of heaven and earth.
I believe in Jesus Christ, his only Son,
our Lord. He was conceived
by the power of the Holy Spirit
and born of the Virgin Mary.
He suffered under Pontius Pilate,
was crucified, died, and was buried.
He descended to the dead.
On the third day he rose again.
He ascended into heaven,
and is seated at the right hand
of the Father.
He will come again
to judge the living and the dead.
I believe in the Holy Spirit,
the holy Catholic Church,
the communion of saints,
the forgiveness of sins,
the resurrection of the body,
and the life everlasting. Amen.

# GUARDIAN ANGEL PRAYER

Angel of God,
my Guardian dear,
to whom God's love
commits me here.
Ever this day
be at my side
to light and guard
to rule and guide.
Amen.

## THE MEMORARE

Remember,
O most gracious Virgin Mary,
that never was it known
that anyone who fled
to your protection,
implored your help or sought your
intercession was left unaided.
Inspired with this confidence,
I fly to you,
O Virgin of virgins, my Mother.
To you I come, before you I stand,
sinful and sorrowful.
O Mother of the Word Incarnate,
do not ignore my petitions,
but in your mercy
hear and answer me. Amen.

# SOUL OF CHRIST

Soul of Christ, sanctify me.
Body of Christ, save me.
Blood of Christ. inebriate me.
Water from the side of Christ,
wash me.

Passion of Christ, strengthen me.
O good Jesus, hear me.
Within your wounds hide me.

Separated from you, let me never be.
From the malignant enemy, defend me.

At the hour of death, call me.
To come to you, bid me,
that I may praise you
in the company of your saints,
for all eternity. Amen.

# Prayer Before a Crucifix

Look down upon me, good and gentle Jesus, while before your face I humbly kneel and with burning soul pray and beg you to fix deep in my heart lively feelings of faith, hope and charity, true contrition for my sins, and a firm purpose of amendment.

While I contemplate, with great love and tender pity, your five most precious wounds, pondering over them within me and calling to mind the words which David, your prophet, said of you, my Jesus:

"They have pierced my hands and my feet, they have numbered all my bones." Amen.

# Beliefs

## THE SACRAMENTS

Baptism

Confirmation

Eucharist

Reconciliation

Anointing of the Sick

Marriage

Holy Orders

# THE BEATITUDES

1. Blessed are the poor in spirit:
   the reign of God is theirs.

2. Blessed are the sorrowing: they shall
   be consoled.

3. ·Blessed are the lowly: they shall
   inherit the land.

4. Blessed are they who hunger
   and thirst for holiness:
   they shall have their fill.

5. Blessed are they who show mercy:
   mercy shall be theirs.

6. Blessed are the single-hearted:
   for they shall see God.

7. Blessed are the peacemakers:
   they shall be called sons of God.

8. Blessed are those persecuted
   for holiness' sake: the reign of God
   is theirs.

# THE WORKS OF MERCY

## The Corporal Works of Mercy
To feed the hungry.
To give drink to the thirsty.
To clothe the naked.
To visit and ransom the captives.
To shelter the homeless.
To visit the sick.
To bury the dead.

## The Spiritual Works of Mercy
To admonish sinners.
To instruct the ignorant.
To counsel the doubtful.
To comfort the sorrowful.
To bear wrongs patiently.
To forgive all injuries.
To pray for the living and the dead.

# THE TEN COMMANDMENTS

1. I, the Lord, am your God. You shall not have other gods besides me.

2. You shall not take the name of the Lord, your God, in vain.

3. Remember to keep holy the Sabbath Day.

4. Honor your father and your mother.

5. You shall not kill.

6. You shall not commit adultery.

7. You shall not steal.

8. You shall not bear false witness against your neighbor.

9. You shall not covet your neighbor's wife.

10. You shall not covet anything that belongs to your neighbor.

# STATIONS OF THE CROSS

**FIRST STATION**  Jesus is Condemned to Death

**SECOND STATION**  Jesus Carries His Cross

**THIRD STATION**  Jesus Falls the First Time

**FOURTH STATION**  Jesus Meets His Afflicted Mother

**FIFTH STATION**  Simon Helps Jesus Carry His Cross

**SIXTH STATION**  Veronica Wipes the Face of Jesus

**SEVENTH STATION**  Jesus Falls the Second Time

**EIGHTH STATION**  Jesus Meets the Women of Jerusalem

**NINTH STATION**  Jesus Falls a Third Time

**TENTH STATION**  Jesus is Stripped of His Clothes

**ELEVENTH STATION**  Jesus is Nailed to the Cross

**TWELFTH STATION**  Jesus Dies on the Cross

**THIRTEENTH STATION**  The Body of Jesus is Taken Down from the Cross

**FOURTEENTH STATION**  Jesus is Laid in the Tomb

# THE ROSARY

## The Joyful Mysteries
1. The Annunciation
2. The Visitation
3. The Nativity
4. The Presentation
5. The Finding in the Temple

## The Sorrowful Mysteries
1. Jesus' Agony in the Garden
2. The Scourging at the Pillar
3. The Crowning with Thorns
4. Jesus Carries His Cross
5. The Crucifixion

## The Glorious Mysteries
1. The Resurrection
2. The Ascension
3. The Descent of the Holy Spirit
4. The Assumption of Mary
5. The Crowning of Mary